Alterna[te] [Tunin]g Guide for Guitar

By Mark Hanson
Introduces eight of the most commonly used guitar tunings.

Interior design and layout by Don Giller
Edited by Peter Pickow and Don Giller

This book Copyright © 1991 by Amsco Publications,
A Division of Music Sales Corporation, New York, NY.

All rights reserved. No part of this book may be
reproduced in any form or by any electronic or mechanical means
including information storage and retrieval systems,
without permission in writing from the publisher.

Exclusive Distributors:
Music Sales Corporation
257 Park Avenue South, New York, NY 10010 USA
Music Sales Limited
8/9 Frith Street, London W1V 5TZ England
Music Sales Pty. Limited
120 Rothschild Street, Rosebery, Sydney, NSW 2018, Australia

Order No. AM 72521
US International Standard Book Number: 0.8256.1251.9
UK International Standard Book Number: 0.7119.1658.6

Printed in the United States of America by
Vicks Lithograph and Printing Corporation

Amsco Publications
New York/London/Sydney

Acknowledgements

I would like to thank all of great guitarists from whom I have learned over the years. Some of them may not have parted with their secrets knowingly (I have spent literally thousands of hours in front of turntables and tape recorders transcribing guitar music), but the effect was the same as if I had been sitting in a room with them.

A special thank you goes to John Renbourn for his insight into the development of alternate tunings in the British Isles. Also to Phil Hood and Jim Hatlo, cohorts at *Frets*, for their support and interest in my publishing projects. And to Jas Obrecht at *Guitar Player* Magazine for sharing the wealth of his knowledge of the blues.

A hearty thank you goes out to Dave McCumiskey and Peter Pickow of Music Sales for their perseverance in this and other projects.

Lastly, I must thank my wife Greta and daughter Marta for their assistance in dealing with a deadline.

Table of Contents

Introduction

Some Practical Matters

This book is designed to give guitarists an understanding of eight of the most commonly used guitar tunings. Before I get to them, I need to state some basic observations about music and the guitar:

1. First, and perhaps most important: Strings often break when you change their tension. I've broken them even while they were being *loosened*. When retuning, make sure that you aim the face of the guitar away from yourself and anyone else nearby. I know a few people who have been seriously hurt after being struck by an exploding string. Also, be careful when restringing your guitar. Brand new strings can break, too.

2. The strings of the guitar are numbered *1* (the highest, or *treble* string) through *6* (the lowest, or *bass* string). Make sure to learn this, or else you'll retune the bass string when I mean the treble, and you'll be writing me letters asking why the tuning doesn't work. I'd love to hear from you, but ...

3. Letter names of the tunings are given in *ascending* order, from the bass string (sixth string) to the treble string (first string). For example, for *G6* tuning (*D G D G B E*), *D* is its lowest-pitched string and *E* is its highest. As with standard tuning, the actual pitches of all alternate tunings range from approximately two octaves below middle *C* to a step or two above middle *C*.

4. The distance, or *interval*, between each guitar fret is one half-step. This is the distance from one key to the next adjacent key on the piano. The interval of two frets on any string is described as one whole-step.

5. The fingers of the fretting hand are numbered in the following manner: the index finger is *1;* the middle finger is *2;* the ring finger is *3;* and the little finger is *4.* The thumb is notated as *T*. Fingerings in the chord diagrams are *suggested* preferences. You may choose to finger some of them differently. That's fine. Be aware, however, that a good guitarist will often know at least two fingerings for each chord. Then he or she can choose the more convenient one when needed.

6. An *open* string means that that string is not to be fretted. It is vibrating at its maximum length.

7. Alternate tunings work beautifully on both steel- and nylon-string guitars. However, for both guitar types but especially for the nylon-string guitar, a retuned string may take a while to settle into its new pitch. It will tend to return toward the pitch and string tension it just left. To prevent this, simply continue to adjust the string until it remains at the new pitch.

A Little History

Alternate guitar tunings are everywhere. From pop balladeer John Denver to heavy-metal icon Jimmy Page of Led Zeppelin, you'll find guitarists using tunings other than "standard."

Some of the biggest hits of pop music have been accompanied by guitars in alternate tunings. James Taylor's "Country Road" uses a simple *Drop-D* tuning. Crosby, Stills and Nash's "Suite: Judy Blue Eyes" uses an *E E E E B E* drone tuning that is far removed from standard.

Joni Mitchell's hits have all used alternate tunings—she has never learned to play in standard tuning. Even the Beatles got into the act with "Dear Prudence" on *The Beatles* (the "White Album") in 1968.

Outside the pop music realm, another group of recently successful recording artists has blazed new trails with their use of alternate tunings. Michael Hedges, Leo Kottke, John Renbourn, Alex de Grassi, and Will Ackerman have raised the status of the solo guitar to a more respected level than that accorded players of earlier generations.

The Windham Hill Phenomenon

The popularity of alternate tunings for guitar exploded during the 1980s with the sales phenomenon of Windham Hill Records. Hedges, de Grassi, and Ackerman brought the sound of retuned steel-string guitars to an audience that had not yet acknowledged it as a significant part of the guitar idiom. Suddenly thousands of players wanted to know the latest Hedges tuning so that they could learn the guitarist's repertoire, and more non-players bought the records simply to soak up the ambience.

As creative and successful as the Windham Hill players have been in the use of alternate tunings in marketing the music, they are simply part of a continuum. They have all been influenced in their development by instrumentalists who began recording more than a decade earlier: Kottke, Renbourn, John Fahey, Davey Graham, and Bert Jansch, as well as pop vocal artists like Mitchell, Stephen Stills, and David Crosby.

But even these inventive artists—of whom many participated in the folk boom of the sixties—didn't start the trend toward alternate tunings. They were carrying on a tradition that had been handed down from (among others) the Mississippi Delta blues guitarists in the early part of the century.

The Blues Connection

Bluesmen like Son House, Robert Johnson, Muddy Waters, and Skip James had often used alternate tunings to facilitate their powerful styles. These and other players used alternate tunings for their slide-guitar playing, which was an attempt to imitate the human voice. Present-day disciples—such as John Hammond, Paul Geremia, and John Mooney—continue that blues tradition.

What about banjo players who have switched to guitar? There was a wholesale changeover from banjo to guitar in the 1920s and 1930s as ragtime gave way to the jazz era. Banjo players, bringing with them their extensive knowledge of banjo tunings, took up the guitar to survive. In fact, the design of the Martin Guitar Company's prized fingerpicking guitar of the 1930s, the fourteen-fret-neck OM model, was suggested by a converted banjo player.

A Picking Paradise

Meanwhile, another rich tradition of alternate guitar tunings was developing far from the sweltering cottonfields of Mississippi and the jazz hotbed of New Orleans: the *slack key* guitar style of the Hawaiian Islands.

The guitar had been brought to the Islands by the ranch hands who had come to help drive the newly introduced cattle herds. Natives like Gabby Pahinui took the instrument and applied their own "laid back" music to it. The result was termed *slack key* for the manner in which the guitars were tuned.

Pahinui was the undisputed king of this fingerpicking guitar style. In fact, Ry Cooder has called Pahinui his favorite guitarist. Raymond Kane is currently the area's most popular slack key performer.

Elizabethan England

Alternate string tunings can be traced as far back as the sixteenth century in late Renaissance Europe. Then the popular guitarlike instruments were the lute and vihuela. These instruments were most often tuned *G C F A D G* (lowest pitch to highest). Classical guitarists today sometimes use a variation of this tuning pattern adapted to the modern guitar. By lowering the pitch of the third string from G to F♯ the same tuning relationship is obtained: *E A D F♯ B E*. The placement of a capo on the third fret brings this *lute tuning* up to the same pitch as the sixteenth-century instruments.

Constant Change

As you can see from this short summary, there is a long history of alternate tunings for the guitar and guitarlike instruments, and likely it will continue. As long as creative musicians are playing the guitar, more tunings will be invented to act as vehicles for ever new musical ideas.

Understanding How Alternate Tunings Work

After a brief introduction to each tuning, I'll show you how to produce the tunings on your guitar. You'll learn which strings to retune and how much to change them. You'll also learn how to make sure that the guitar is in tune once you have retuned it.

A word of advice is in order here: If you have trouble tuning your guitar nicely by ear, consider buying a *chromatic* tuning machine—one that will read any of the twelve notes of the chromatic scale. This will help you immensely as you deal with the different notes of these various tunings.

While some tunings are more versatile than others, most tunings lend themselves better to playing in one particular key. For each of the eight tunings, I have included a *do-re-mi* scale of the most commonly used key.

These scales are written in both standard music notation and guitar tablature. The tablature demonstrates the *first-position* (end-of-the-neck) fretboard location of the scale notes. If you can't read tablature, study the tablature explanation in the back of the book.

The Good and Bad of Tablature

Understand that the standard music notation of these scales may not change from one tuning to the next, *but the tablature will*. For example, a D major scale has the same pitches (*D, E, F♯*, and so on) no matter what guitar tuning you are using, and so the music notation will not change. But when you retune a string, the *locations* of the notes on that string change.

Let's use *Drop-D* tuning (*D A D G B E*, lowest pitch to highest) as an example. To produce *Drop-D* on the guitar, lower the sixth (lowest bass) string one whole-step below standard tuning. Now the open sixth string is a *D* note instead of an *E*. The *E* note is now located at the second fret. In fact, all of the notes on the bass string in *Drop-D* are located two frets higher than they are in standard tuning.

Retuning a string affects not only the location of the notes but also chord formations. For example, to play a first-position E minor chord in *Drop-D* tuning, you need to finger the regular E minor chord on the second fret of the fourth, fifth, and sixth strings. As noted above, the second fret on the sixth string provides the low *E*. Tablature tells you where to fret that low *E*; standard notation does not.

Some publishers use *only* tablature when printing guitar music in alternate tunings, especially when the tunings are far removed from standard tuning. Few guitarists know where the actual pitches are in alternate tunings, so the publishers save space by deleting the standard notation.

Granted, it does save space. But it prevents other instrumentalists from sightreading the music. It also keeps guitarists from learning an alternate tuning piece in *standard* tuning. Some alternate tunings pieces are actually quite playable in standard—or a less altered— tuning. In addition, tablature cannot notate the duration of notes. A combination of the two systems is preferable.

Additional Ups and Downs of Tunings

Occasionally the tunings listed in this book are raised or lowered somewhat to facilitate the vocalist's singing range or to produce a brighter or deeper tone. For example, many blues players use *Open A* tuning instead of *Open G*, which is listed here. The relationship of the strings to one another are the same; the pitches are simply all one whole-step higher in *Open A*.

The extra tension on the strings in *Open A* tuning (or *Open E* above *Open D*) provides a very bright tone. But it is also hard on the structural integrity of most instruments. To play in *Open A* or *Open E*, consider tuning to *Open G* or *Open D*, respectively, and use a capo at the second fret. If you must tune to *Open A* or *E*, use lighter gauge strings.

Early recordings of Leo Kottke and some of Bahaman guitarist Joseph Spence offer good examples of alternate tunings that are lower than their cousins. Kottke's studio version of "Louise" is in *Drop-C*, while a live version is in *Drop-B♭*. Both tunings use the same string relationships as *Drop-D*, but the entire guitar is tuned down another one or two whole-steps from *Drop-D*. Spence also recorded in *Drop-C* (*C G C F A D*).

New Fingerings

"The difficult thing about tunings is that every time you come up with a new one you have to invent all your fingerings all over again." So said David Crosby in an interview published in *Frets* magazine (July, 1988).

It's true that each new tuning has different chord fingerings. But I have designed this book to introduce you first to tunings that require only minor changes to standard-tuning fingerings. As you progress through the book you will encounter tunings that require more substantial fingering alterations.

We will begin with standard tuning as a common starting place. Then we will move to tunings that alter only one or two strings from standard. In this book, none of the main tunings requires you to retune more than four strings.

A piece of advice: Notice the chord fingerings you use in each new tuning. Often a new tuning might use some familiar fingerings from another tuning. Most likely the old fingering in the new tuning will sound different or will be placed in another location on the fretboard. By noticing that a fingering in a new tuning looks familiar, you will remember it more easily.

Have fun with these alternate tunings. For many people, they open up a whole new world of possibilities on the guitar. And, as David Crosby points out, "the harmonies you can get are worth the effort."

The Tunings

Standard Tuning: E A D G B E

Most guitarists start with standard tuning when they learn to play guitar, and most continue with it for the duration of their picking careers. Of course, there are exceptions: Joni Mitchell, as I mentioned previously, has never played in standard tuning, and Joseph Spence, has played only in *Drop-D* tuning. But most of us start with standard tuning as our home base.

The advantages of standard tuning are numerous. It provides for:

1. standardized, relatively easy fingerings;
2. a wealth of available teaching material; and
3. access to copious amounts of printed music.

The disadvantages of alternate tunings are more numerous:

1. There is a limited number of teaching aids.
2. There exists a small amount of printed material.
3. The player must learn new fingerings for each tuning.
4. If retuned regularly, the strings break or lose their brilliance more quickly than normal.
5. The act of tuning is difficult enough for many players. The thought of retuning from standard can be daunting.

This situation makes one understand why many players never experiment with alternate tunings. At the same time, in my opinion, the challenge is worth the effort.

To Produce Standard Tuning

The easiest way to produce standard tuning on your guitar is to match the bass-string *E* to an *E* tuning fork, pitch pipe, piano, or another fixed-pitch source. Then tune the guitar by matching the fifth-fret note on each string to the adjacent, higher-pitched open string.

The only exception to this fifth-fret rule is the third string: Fret the third string at the *fourth* fret to match the pitch of the open second string. (Remember that the second string is an unwound *treble* string, not a bass string!)

Take a look at the following tuning diagram. It shows the fretboard locations that will produce standard tuning using the fifth-fret tuning technique. The pitch of each fretted note in the diagram equals the adjacent higher-pitched open string.

Getting in Tune

There are several ways to make sure your guitar is correctly in standard tuning. First, there is the "Here Comes the Bride" method.

Play the bass string once, then the fifth string three times, in the rhythm of "Here Comes the Bride." If the two strings are in tune, they should sound like the traditional bridal march tune. If it doesn't sound like "Here Comes the Bride," go back to your fifth-fret tuning technique and try again.

Once the two bass strings are in tune, do the same thing with the fifth and fourth strings: Pick the fifth string once, then the fourth string three times. Does it sound like "Here Comes the Bride"? It should if they are in tune.

This method works for every pair of strings except the second and third strings. For these two, try this: Play the second string three times, then the third string once, using the rhythm of the beginning to Beethoven's *Fifth Symphony*. (You know that one: "Dah-dah-dah-dum.")

If that doesn't work, try this: Play the fourth string, second string and third string in that order, using an even rhythm. Television watchers will recognize this as the NBC logo, the music behind the peacock.

This is called *ear training*. You already know what "Here Comes the Bride" and "NBC" should sound like; your ears have been trained to hear that. Now apply it to the guitar.

Of course, if you don't like traditional wedding music, you can choose some other tune that starts with the same interval (a *perfect fourth* interval, the distance from the first note to the fourth note of a *do-re-mi* scale). The first notes of "Columbia, the Gem of the Ocean," "Dust in the Wind," or the end-of-the-day bugle call "Taps" will work just as well.

Harmonics

A second method for checking tuning uses harmonics. In standard tuning, the fifth-fret harmonic on any string should equal the seventh-fret harmonic on the adjacent higher-pitched string—with one exception, which I will address shortly.

A quick lesson on harmonics: Lightly touch—but don't push down—the sixth string directly above the fifth fretwire. Sharply pick the bass string. You should produce a ringing tone two octaves above the open bass string. Do the same thing at the seventh fret of the fifth string. You should produce the same note.

Continue toward the treble strings: The fifth-fret harmonic of the fifth string equals the seventh-fret harmonic of the fourth string; the fifth-fret harmonic of the fourth string equals the seventh-fret harmonic of the third, and so on.

As in the fifth-fret tuning technique, the only exception is the third and second strings. Their harmonics will not produce the same note. Use the first tuning method for these two strings.

If you have trouble producing harmonics, practice at the twelfth fret. Harmonics are easier to produce there. Make sure you pick the string sharply (use a "rest stroke" about two inches from the bridge), and use a relaxed left hand to lightly touch the string *directly above* the twelfth fretwire.

Electronic Tuners

Finally, you can use an electronic tuner to get nicely in tune. But I agree with Leo Kottke when he states, "They erase my ear." Tuning is a great way to practice ear training—teaching your ear to hear what the intervals are supposed to sound like.

Electronic tuners certainly have their place. There may be no other way to get in tune if you are in a noisy room. But try to use your ear instead of a tuner as much as you can. You will be a more discerning listener and musician because of it.

D Major Scale

When in standard tuning, most guitarists are comfortable playing in five major keys: A, C, D, E, and G. Most or all of the open-string notes are members of these keys, and they can be used easily. I have illustrated by example the D major scale, so that you can compare the locations of the notes with the D tunings in the following sections.

The scale begins on the second degree, the *E*, which is the lowest available note on the open sixth string. It continues up to high *G*, the third fret of the first string. Play this scale both ascending and descending to get a feel for where the notes lie on the fretboard.

Pay close attention to the locations of the notes notated in the tablature. These positions will change when you retune one or more of your strings.

D Major Scale

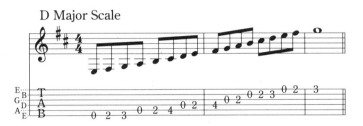

Common Chord Fingerings

Illustrated below are many of the most commonly used major, minor, and dominant-seventh chords in each tuning. These standard-tuning fingerings are likely very familiar to you.

Remember that these chord fingerings are suggested ones. You may finger these chords differently if you prefer. But make your fingering decisions based on thought, not whim.

As with the D major scale, make sure you are familiar with these chords so that you have a basis for comparison as you begin retuning strings.

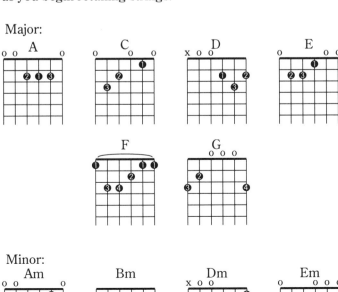

11

Dominant Sevenths:

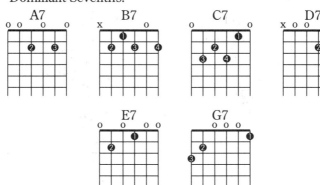

Recordings That Use Standard Tuning

Included in the following list are some of the best-known songs with notable guitar parts that are in standard tuning. The list contains the artist, the song title, and the album on which the song appears.

Beatles	"Here Comes the Sun"
	Abbey Road
Blind Blake	"Diddie Wa Diddie"
	Search Warrant Blues, Vol. 2
John Denver	"Take Me Home, Country Roads"
	Greatest Hits, Vol. 1
Donovan	"Jennifer, Juniper"
	Greatest Hits
Fleetwood Mac	"Landslide"
	Fleetwood Mac
	"Oh, Well"
	Then Play On
Dan Fogelberg	"Leader of the Band"
	Greatest Hits
Arlo Guthrie	"Alice's Restaurant"
	Alice's Restaurant
Heart	"Crazy on You"
	Dreamboat Annie
Kansas	"Dust in the Wind"
	Point of Know Return
Leo Kottke	"Fisherman"
	6- & 12- String Guitar
Led Zeppelin	"Stairway to Heaven"
	Led Zeppelin IV
Don McLean	"Vincent"
	American Pie
Paul Simon	"Scarborough Fair"
	Parsley, Sage, Rosmary and Tyme
Bruce Springsteen	"I'm on Fire"
	Born in the U.S.A.
James Taylor	"Fire and Rain"
	James Taylor
Merle Travis	"Nine Pound Hammer"
	Hillbilly Music...Thank God!, Vol. 1
Edward Van Halen	"Spanish Fly"
	Van Halen 2
Dave Van Ronk	"Cocaine Blues"
	Dave Van Ronk
Mason Williams	"Classical Gas"
	Phonograph Record
Neil Young	"Needle and the Damage Done"
	Harvest

Drop-D Tuning: D A D G B E

If you haven't worked with alternate guitar tunings before, *Drop-D* tuning is the first alternate tuning to explore. There are three main reasons to start with Drop-D:

1. It is easy to produce—it requires only one string to be retuned from standard tuning.
2. Most of the chord fingerings are the same as in standard tuning.
3. Drop-D provides an added richness to the guitar.

Because of its ease of use and its rich sound, Drop-D is the most commonly used alternate tuning among guitarists. Joseph Spence liked Drop-D so much that he recorded with it exclusively. (See the recording list at the end of this section.)

To Produce Drop-D Tuning
Only one alteration is made from standard tuning to produce Drop-D: the sixth string is tuned down one whole-step, from *E* to *D*. Most standard-tuning chord formations will not change.

To produce low *D* on a steel-string guitar, you will have to turn the tuning machine approximately one-third turn. On a nylon-string guitar you may have to turn the tuning peg a bit more.

Getting in Tune
Several methods are used to make sure the sixth string is in tune, once it is lowered to *D*. The seventh-fret note on the sixth string should be an *A*, the same pitch as the open fifth string. Also, play the note (or the harmonic) at the twelfth fret on the sixth string. It should be the same pitch as the open fourth string, a *D*.

Once the guitar is in tune, play a first-position D chord using all six strings. The guitar should sound richer and fuller than the same D chord fingering in standard tuning.

You now have a D chord with the lowest root note on the sixth string instead of the fourth, an octave below the lowest root note of the standard-tuning D chord. The low *D* note provides the added richness in the Drop-D version. (The root note of a chord is the note the chord on which it is built. This, the root note of a D chord is a *D*.)

The following tuning diagram shows the fret on each string where the pitch matches the adjacent higher-pitched, unfretted string. All of the locations are identical to standard tuning except the sixth string, where you use the seventh fret.

D Major Scale
It's only natural that the most commonly used key in Drop-D tuning is D major. The root note of the tonic chord is the lowest note in the bass, and it lends a rich finality to any chord progression that ends on the I chord (D).

But D major is certainly not the only key guitarists use in this tuning. D minor and G major are other common keys.

There are a number of published tunes that use Drop-D for the key of G major, including my piece "Ryan Time (Again)" that was featured in the August 1989 issue of *Frets* magazine. (For back issues and other sources of printed and recorded guitar music, see "Sources" in the back of this book.) The low D note of this tuning gives the dominant-seventh chord of G (a D7) an added richness that resolves nicely to a G chord.

For purposes of comparison, we will stick with the key of D major for the scale diagram. Note that the first *four* notes of the scale are on the bass string in Drop-D, while only three were on the sixth string in standard tuning. Also, notice the frets you use on the sixth string in Drop-D are different from standard tuning. The positions on the other five strings are identical to standard tuning.

D Major Scale

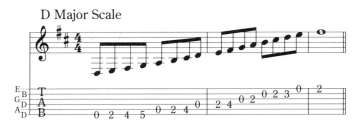

Common Chord Fingerings

Shown below are common chord fingerings for Drop-D tuning. Many are the same as in standard tuning. The bass string offers the exception. As we have seen, you may strum all six strings now when playing a common D fingering. It will sound great. To play an E chord (major, minor, or dominant seventh), you have to fret the bass string at the *second* fret. (If you use your thumb to fret the sixth string, you might play a standard-tuning E fingering, with the thumb fretting the bass string.)

Take a look at the G chord. It looks like a regular G7 fingering moved up two frets. This illustrates familiar-looking fingerings in new tunings.

However, be careful of the fifth string if you equate the new G chord to a G7 fingering. If you finger an regular G7 chord at the fifth, fourth, and third frets, you'll get a sour note on the fifth string. Add your little finger at the fifth fret of the fifth string, or mute the fifth string with the flesh of your ring finger as it frets the sixth string.

Consider excluding the sixth string from your strumming or picking on chords such as C and B7. Those low notes are unnecessary, and they make for cumbersome fingering.

Major:

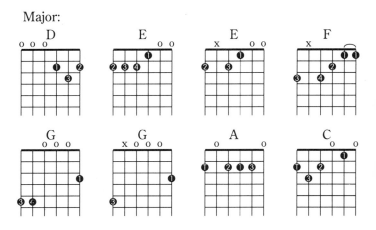

Minor:

Dm

Em

F#m

Am

Bm
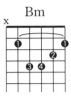

Dominant Sevenths:

D7

E7
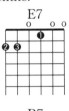
G7

A7

B7

C7

Recordings That Use Drop-D Tuning

There are thousands of recordings that include Drop-D tuning. Here is a representative list covering a variety of styles.

The Band	"Jemima Surrender"
	The Band
Beatles	"Dear Prudence"
	The Beatles (the "White Album")
Ry Cooder	"FDR in Trinidad"
	Into the Purple Valley
David Crosby	"Everybody's Been Burned"
	Byrds - Younger Than Yesterday
D. Crosby, G. Nash	"Carry Me"
	Wind on the Water
Peppino D'Agostino	"Lagavullin"
	Acoustic Spirit
	"Bossa for Francesco"
	Acoustic Spirit
Alex de Grassi	"Children's Dance"
	Turning: Turning Back
	"Overland"
	Southern Exposure
John Denver	"Poems, Prayers and Promises"
	"Rocky Mountain High"
	Greatest Hits, Vol. 1
Doobie Brothers	"Black Water"
	Best of the Doobies
	"Mamaloi"
	Toulouse Street
Rik Emmett	"Midsummer's Daydream"
	Thunder Seven
Mark Hanson	"Ryan Time (Again)"
	Waterwheel

Bert Jansch	"Ramblin's Gonna Be the Death of Me"
	Lucky 13
Jorma Kaukonen	"Embryonic Journey"
	Surrealistic Pillow
Leo Kottke	"Louise"
	Greenhouse
	"Mona Ray"
	The Best
	"Little Beaver"
	A Shout Toward Noon
	"Shortwave"
	Regards from Chuck Pink
	"Everybody Lies"
	My Father's Face
Led Zeppelin	"Going To California"
	Zeppelin 4
Don McLean	"Castles In The Air"
	Tapestry
	"Three Flights Up"
	Tapestry
John Renbourn	"The Hermit"
	The Hermit
	"Sweet Potato"
	Sir John Alot of…
	"Lady Goes To Church"
	Sir John Alot of…
Pete Seeger	"Livin' in the Country"
	Greatest Hits
Bola Sete	"Let Go"
	"Vira Mundo Penba"
	Ocean
Joseph Spence	"Glory, Glory"
	Folk Guitar
James Taylor	"Country Road"
	James Taylor
	"Lighthouse"
	Gorilla
	"Millworker"
	Flag
	"Sugar Trade"
	Dad Loves His Work

Double Drop-D: D A D G B D

A second alternate tuning that is relatively close to standard tuning is *Double Drop-D*. It is also called *Double-D-Down*.

I first came across this tuning while listening to Stephen Stills play his acoustic guitar solo on "Bluebird" (from *Buffalo Springfield Again*). The Drop-D on the sixth string was obvious on the recording, but at the end of the instrumental section Stills strummed a Cmaj9 chord that was impossible to produce in standard tuning: the highest pitched note was a *D*, a whole-step below the normal open-first-string note.

With a little experimentation I discovered that Stills's Cmaj9 chord and the rest of his instrumental on "Blue-bird" could be reproduced by dropping the first string—along with the sixth—to *D*.

Stills and bandmate Neil Young apparently shared an early interest in Double Drop-D tuning. Young's solo recording career, which began shortly after the *Buffalo Springfield Again* album, has included several songs using *D A D G B D* tuning. Buffy St. Marie is another artist who uses this tuning.

To Produce Double Drop-D

Begin by tuning to Drop-D: lower the sixth string a whole-step to *D*. Now do the same thing to the first (treble) string: lower it one whole-step to *D*.

To make sure the first string is in tune, fret the second string at the third fret. That note, a *D*, should match the open first string. Another way to check the tuning is to play the twelfth-fret note (or harmonic) on the fourth string. That note is also a *D*, the same pitch as the open first string.

The following tuning diagram shows where to fret on each string to match the adjacent higher-pitched unfretted string.

D Major Scale

The D major scale in Double Drop-D looks the same as Drop-D until you get to the second string. You can switch to the first string sooner in Double Drop-D.

Play the scale ascending and descending several times to get it "in your fingers."

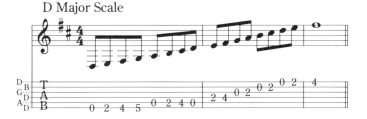

D Major Scale

Common Chord Fingerings

With Double Drop-D tuning, you have the freedom to enhance your chords with very little effort. A beautiful Cadd9 chord is fingered just like a regular C in standard tuning. The open first string provides the added ninth.

Aadd11 is a beautiful chord as well, once you get accustomed to the dissonance. These kinds of chords allow you to play partial scales without moving any fingers in the left hand.

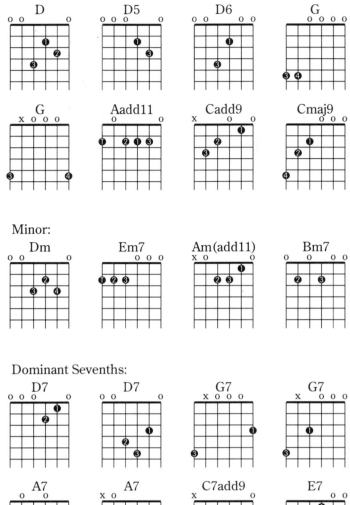

Major:
D   D5   D6   G
G   Aadd11   Cadd9   Cmaj9

Minor:
Dm   Em7   Am(add11)   Bm7

Dominant Sevenths:
D7   D7   G7   G7
A7   A7   C7add9   E7

Recordings That Use Double Drop-D

There are not as many recordings of Double Drop-D as there are of other tunings, but those that exist do not lack in quality.

Peter Finger	"Petermann's Polka"
	Acoustic Folk Rock
Mark Hanson	"Strawberry Curl"
	Solo Style (book/cassette)
Stephen Stills	"Bluebird"
	Buffalo Springfield Again
Neil Young	"Cinnamon Girl"
	Everybody Knows This Is Nowhere
	"When You Dance I Can Really Love"
	After the Gold Rush

D A D G A D Tuning

This tuning was developed by English fingerstyle guitarist Davey Graham in the early sixties. To many people, Graham is best known as the composer of the instrumental "Anji," which Paul Simon recorded on Simon & Garfunkel's *Sounds Of Silence* album.

Graham came up with the *DADGAD* (pronounced "Dad Gad") tuning while accompanying *oud* players in Morocco. Since then, the tuning has become a favorite among British players of traditional music. Even Led Zeppelin's Jimmy Page has recorded traditional British music on an acoustic guitar using DADGAD. His "Black Mountain Side" from the first Led Zeppelin album is a DADGAD instrumental version of the traditional tune "Black Water Side."

Another English guitar virtuoso, John Renbourn, has admitted his attraction to this tuning because of its potential for fine melodic playing, supported by an accompaniment of droning open strings.

With all this English interest in the tuning, it is interesting that a Frenchman—Pierre Bensusan—has become the leading exponent of DADGAD. His grasp of the tuning is as complete as any virtuoso's understanding of standard tuning. Bensusan will often play an entire concert without changing from DADGAD.

To Produce DADGAD

To alter the tuning of your strings: DADGAD is one step beyond Double Drop-D. Lower your first and sixth strings one whole-step to *D*. Check them as you did for Double Drop-D: The seventh-fret note of the sixth string equals the open fifth string, and the third-fret note of the second string equals the open first.

Next, lower the open second string one whole-step to *A*. To check the tuning of the second string, the third string at the second fret should equal the open second string. Note that once you tune both the first and second strings down, the *fifth* fret of the second string will equal the open first string.

The tuning diagram below shows the fretted position of each string that matches the adjacent higher-pitched open string.

You can also check your tuning using harmonics. The harmonic at the twelfth fret of the sixth string should equal the open fourth string. The harmonic at the twelfth fret of the fourth string should equal the open first string. These three strings are all D's. To make sure your A strings (second and fifth) are in tune, compare the twelfth-fret harmonic of the fifth string to the open second string.

D Major Scale

In DADGAD, the positions of the D Major scale notes stray far from their original positions in standard tuning. Play the scale up and down to get comfortable with the positions.

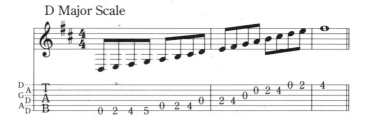

D Major Scale

Common Chord Fingerings

As noted above, DADGAD is often used for melodic playing, with open drone strings providing the harmonic accompaniment. You may surmise that there are not many chord fingerings for DADGAD. Not so. Page's "Black Mountain Side" begins with a melodic fragment, but it is quickly supported by two- and three-finger chords. A transcription of "Black Mountain Side" is available from Acoustic Classics (see "Sources").

Experiment with the chord fingerings below. Often, the beauty of these tunings lies in the additional notes you can include in your chords besides the standard 1-3-5. Be creative. Look for the ninths, sixths, and elevenths. Close dissonances in these tunings is what often gives them their unique character.

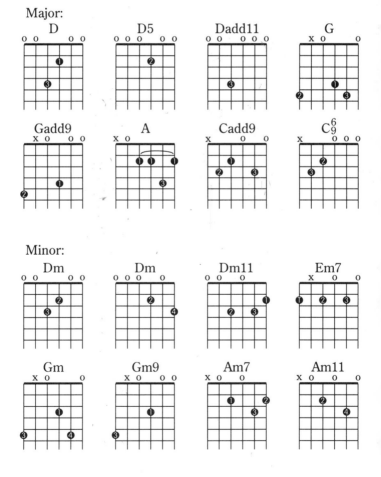

Dominant Sevenths:

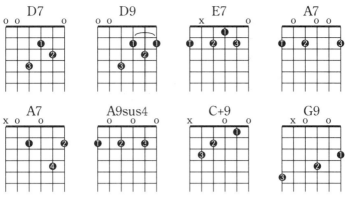

Recordings That Use DADGAD Tuning

There are many virtuoso DADGAD tunes in print, including a complete book by Pierre Bensusan.

A very musical scale exercise in DADGAD is Martin Simpson's arrangement of "Garryowen" (published in *Frets*, September 1986). The opening of the tune is a D major scale descending one octave from D to D. Legend has it that this tune was General George Custer's marching tune.

Pierre Bensusan	"Four A.M."
	Spices
	"Jesu, Joy Of Man's Desiring"
	The Guitar Book (book)
	"Last Pint"
	Spices
	"Solilai"
	Solilai
Peppino D'Agostino	"The Genie"
	Acoustic Spirit
Stefan Grossman	"Woman From Donori"
	Snap a Little Owl
Mark Hanson	"Twin Sisters"
	Solo Style (book/cassette)
Michael Hedges	"Peg Leg Speed King"
	Breakfast in the Field
	"Ragamuffin"
	Aerial Boundaries
Bert Jansch	"So Long (Been on the Road So Long)"
	Lucky 13
Jimmy Page	"Black Mountain Side"
	Led Zeppelin
John Renbourn	"A Maid That's Deep in Love"
	A Maid That's Deep in Love
	"House Carpenter"
	Pentangle: Basket of Light
	"Kemp's Jig"
	Frets (magazine—December '88)
Martin Simpson	"Garryowen"
	Nobody's Fault But Mine

Open D (or D major) Tuning: D A D F♯ A D

Joni Mitchell is the most notable contemporary guitarist associated with this rich, ringing tuning. Songs from her early recordings, like "Big Yellow Taxi" and "Chelsea Morning," use *Open D* tuning.

Easy fingerings, a tonic-to-tonic melodic range on the first string (*D* to *D* in the key of D), and the use of all the open strings have attracted many players to this tuning. Duane Allman and Dickie Betts of the Allman Bothers stepped out of their Dixie rock style to record a beautiful acoustic fingerstyle duet, "Little Martha," in Open D's cousin *Open E*. To produce Open E, either tune everything up one whole-step from Open D, or simply capo Open D at the second fret. Leo Kottke also recorded an Open D version of "Little Martha," but in *Open C♯*! He tuned everything down one half-step from Open D. Kottke was especially well known early in his career for producing a throaty roar from his twelve-string guitar in Open C tuning—Open D but with all strings lowered one whole-step. Other fingerstyle instrumentalists like Peter Lang, Alex de Grassi, and Will Ackerman use it as well. (See record sources at the end of this section.)

Open D tuning is also popular among blues players, especially those who play slide guitar. As mentioned previously, bluesman Robert Johnson used Open E, which is the same as Open D except one whole-step higher. Ry Cooder's Open D slide rendition of Chuck Berry's romping "Thirteen Question Method" was published in the June, 1989, issue of *Frets*.

Since Open E puts more stress on the guitar than Open D, you might consider using light-gauge strings if you plan to tune to Open E.

To Produce Open D

From standard tuning, follow the same tuning procedure as DADGAD: Lower the first, second, and sixth strings one whole-step. Then, lower the third string one half-step to *F♯*.

To check the results, first make sure your three D strings (first, fourth, and sixth) are in tune by producing twelfth-fret harmonics on the sixth and fourth strings. Second, check your A strings (second and fifth) by using the twelfth-fret harmonic on the fifth string.

Finally, compare your open third string (F♯) the fourth fret of the fourth string. The pitches should be the same.

Here is the tuning diagram to show you the fretted positions used for tuning in *Open D*.

D Major Scale

This is as far from standard-tuning fingering for a D major scale as we will get in this book. Only two strings remain the same: the fourth and the fifth.

Play this one enough times to get a feel for it. By now you are developing some of the mental and physical dexterity common to all good alternate tunings players.

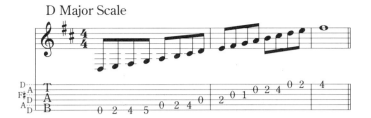

D Major Scale

Common Chord Fingerings

Joni Mitchell's early songs are good examples for basic chord formations in Open D tuning. For example, a first-position E-chord fingering in standard tuning is beautiful in Open D if well placed. Mitchell plays it in first position to produce a chord that may be called A9sus4/D or Em11/D. She also plays it in third position to produce a Dmaj7.

Major chords are simply barred straight across the strings, with no added fingers. Those of you who dislike bar chords will appreciate that.

Don't be afraid to use the open first and second strings as drones while you chord on the four bass strings. It can have a beautiful effect.

Recordings That Use Open D Tuning

You'll find this tuning in many styles. It's great for everything from powerful strumming to slide to delicate fingerpicking.

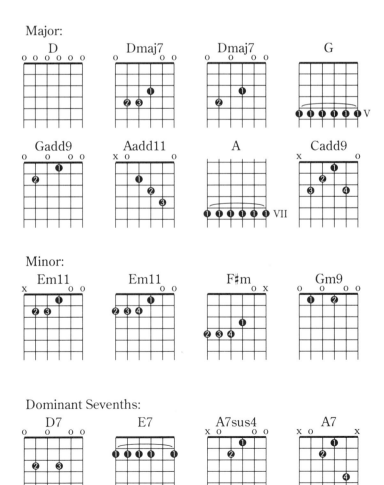

Major:
D   Dmaj7   Dmaj7   G

Gadd9   Aadd11   A   Cadd9

Minor:
Em11   Em11   F#m   Gm9

Dominant Sevenths:
D7   E7   A7sus4   A7

Will Ackerman	"Ely"
	Search for the Turtle's Navel
Allman Brothers	"Little Martha"
	Eat a Peach
Robbie Basho	"Variations On Easter"
	Visions of the Country
Ry Cooder	"Thirteen Question Method"
	Get Rhythm
Alex de Grassi	"Alpine Medley"
	Turning: Turning Back
Robert Johnson	"Preachin' Blues"
	The Complete Recordings
Tommie Johnson	"Lonesome Home Blues"
	Jackson Blues
Leo Kottke	"Little Martha"
	A Shout Toward Noon
	"Watermelon"
	6- & 12-String Guitar
Peter Lang	"As I Lay Sleeping"
	Leo Kottke/Peter Lang/John Fahey
David Lindley	"Look So Good"
	Win This Record
Joni Mitchell	"Big Yellow Taxi"
	Clouds
	"Chelsea Morning"
	Ladies of the Canyon

Open G Tuning: D G D G B D

Players from such disparate styles as raunchy country blues to blissful new age have used this versatile tuning. Most of the great blues slide guitarists have favored *Open G* during their careers. As we know from his recordings on Columbia Records, Robert Johnson used it extensively. Muddy Waters spent much of the early part of his career playing slide guitar in Open G. To play in other keys, Waters simply maintained Open G tuning and used a capo. Both Johnson and Waters were influenced by the open-tuning playing and songwriting of the great Son House.

With string tension in mind, blues player John Mooney uses Open G on his heavier-strung acoustic guitar and the higher-pitched *Open A* on his lightly-strung electric.

As with Open D, Open G is used extensively by fingerstyle guitarists. Leo Kottke has recorded many of his powerful twelve-string instrumentals using Open G. Jorma Kaukonen plays one of his rhythm-heavy instrumentals, "Water Song," in this tuning. Led Zeppelin's Jimmy Page uses Open G as well in "Bron-Y-Aur Stomp," among other tunes.

Open G is also a common banjo tuning. If you delete the sixth and fifth strings of the tuning (D and A) and add a high G as the banjo's fifth string, you have Open G on the five-string banjo.

In fact, Keith Richard of the Rolling Stones calls Open G a banjo tuning. To produce it on his guitar, he actually takes the sixth string off. Then he tunes to Open G, with the fifth string a low-pitched *G* instead of the high *G* of the banjo. In this way the root note of the tonic chord, *G*, is the lowest bass note. It still has all of the advantages of Open G tuning that so attracted the early blues guitarists.

To Produce Open G Tuning

You may not realize it, but in standard tuning you already have three open strings that together produce a G chord. The open second, third and fourth strings (B, G, and D) are the three notes of a G major chord. Try hitting a twelfth-fret harmonic simultaneously on these three strings. It's a beautiful sound.

Now you need to retune the other three. Lower your sixth and first strings to *D*, as you did for Double Drop-D. Then lower your *fifth* string one whole-step to *G*.

Check your harmonics to match the three D strings. The twelfth-fret harmonic of the fifth string (now a *G*) should match your open third string. Also, the seventh-fret note of the fifth string should now equal the fourth string.

This tuning diagram shows you the locations of the fretted notes to use in tuning.

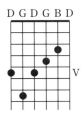

G Major Scale

One attraction of this tuning for many players is the range of the melody on the first string. While Open D has a range from *do* to *do* (the first note of the D scale up to an octave up), Open G has a range from *so* to *so* (the fifth note of the scale to the octave above). Keep that in mind when you use this string (especially in slide playing) to imitate the vocal melody.

The locations of the notes shouldn't take too much time to master if you have practiced with Double Drop-D. Only the fifth string is tuned differently.

G Major Scale

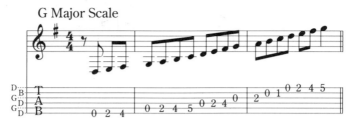

Common Chord Fingerings

As you have been discovering, open strings can be used as extra notes to spice up your basic 1-3-5 chords in open tunings. Open G is no exception.

Some of the minor chords are especially nice in Open G. The A minor chords with the added eleventh have a particularly haunting sound. You'll find the Bm (add♭6) in Randy Scruggs's arrangement of "Both Sides Now."

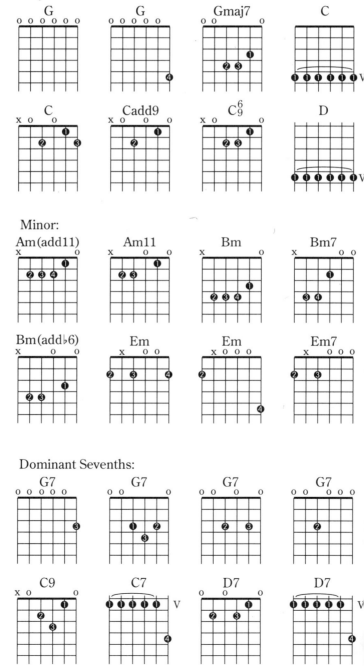

26

Recordings That Use Open G Tuning

Some of the greatest guitarists have made their livings off Open G tuning. Even alternate-tunings virtuoso Michael Hedges uses it. I especially recommend that you listen to some of the early blues guitarists if you are not already familiar with them. They can make this tuning scream, even without hundreds of watts of power burning behind them.

Ry Cooder	"Available Space"
	Available Space
Dan Fogelberg	"Longer"
	Phoenix
Nanci Griffith	"Love at the Five and Dime"
	One Fair Summer Evening
John Hammond	"Drop Down Mama"
	Best of John Hammond
Michael Hedges	"Eleven Small Roaches"
	Breakfast in the Field
Robert Johnson	"Milkcow's Calf Blues"
	"Travelin' Riverside"
	"Walkin' Blues"
	The Complete Recordings
Jorma Kaukonen	"Water Song"
	Burgers
Leo Kottke	"Jack Fig"
	"Jesu, Joy Of Man's Desiring"
	6- & 12-String Guitar
	"Machine 3"
	The Best
Mance Lipscomb	"Joe Turner Killed a Man"
	Texas Songster, Vol. 2
Jimmy Page	"Bron-Y-Aur Stomp"
	Physical Graffiti
Chris Proctor	"Huckleberry Hornpipe"
	Delicate Dance
Bonnie Raitt	"Write Me a Few of Your Lines"
	Takin' My Time
John Renbourn	"Old Mac Bladgitt"
	The Hermit
Randy Scruggs	"Both Sides Now"
	"Amazing Grace"
	Will the Circle Be Unbroken
Martin Simpson	"Charlie's Boogie"
	Nobody's Fault But Mine
James Taylor	"Love Has Brought Me Around"
	Mud Slide Slim

G6 Tuning: D G D G B E

G6 tuning (also called *Drop-G*) is a wonderful and easy way of playing in the key of G. It is an especially nice tuning for playing pieces that are intricate melodically, such as fiddle tunes.

The fifth and sixth strings are each tuned down one whole-step to a *G* and a *D*, respectively. Now the root notes of the tonic (*G*) and dominant (*D*) chords appear on open strings in the bass, so there is little need to fret them with the left hand. This in turn leaves the left hand free to deal with melody notes on the treble strings.

The other nice aspect of G6 tuning is that the four treble strings remain identical to standard tuning, so many of the standard-tuning chord formations are not altered.

Chet Atkins has used G6 tuning very effectively in a number of his recordings. "Yellow Bird" and "Vincent" are two notable examples.

I use G6 tuning for a fingerstyle arrangement of the fiddle tune "Devil's Dream" in my *Solo Style* book. Since my arrangement has only three chords (G, D, and Am) and can actually be played with just two (G and D), I never fret the sixth string and I seldom fret the fifth. This gives my left hand the freedom to fret the running eighth-note melody on the treble strings over an alternating bass that is played almost entirely on open strings.

By capoing the guitar at the second fret, I can play "Devil's Dream" right along with the fiddlers who normally play it in the key of A.

To Produce G6 Tuning

To produce G6 tuning from standard, first lower the sixth string one whole-step to *D* (exactly like Drop-D tuning). At this point, the seventh-fret note of the sixth string should equal the open fifth string.

Next, lower the fifth string one whole-step to *G*. Now the seventh-fret note of the fifth string should equal the open fourth string. Note that once you have tuned both strings down, the *fifth-fret* note of the sixth string should equal the open fifth string.

Check the tuning of the two bass strings with harmonics as well. The twelfth-fret harmonic of the sixth string should equal the pitch of the open fourth string. The twelfth-fret harmonic of the open fifth string should equal the open third string.

The tuning diagram below will help you find the fretted notes that you use to tune the strings.

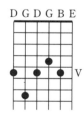

G Major Scale

Except for the two bass strings, both standard and G6 tuning use the same G major scale The location of the scale notes on the two bass strings correspond to Open G tuning.

This is a nice tuning for playing scales on the treble strings, which makes it a good tuning for everything from fiddle tunes to string-bending rock-and-roll licks. Many players are very familiar with these scales in standard tuning. G6 tuning allows the player to use that familiarity on the four treble strings (where most of the lead-guitar work is done anyway), while giving easy "no-fingers" access to accompaniment notes on the two bass strings.

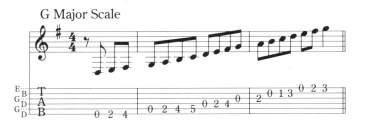

G Major Scale

Common Chord Fingerings

These chord fingerings should look pretty familiar by now. Many of them are ones you already know from standard tuning. Only the sixth- and fifth-string positions are different.

Major:

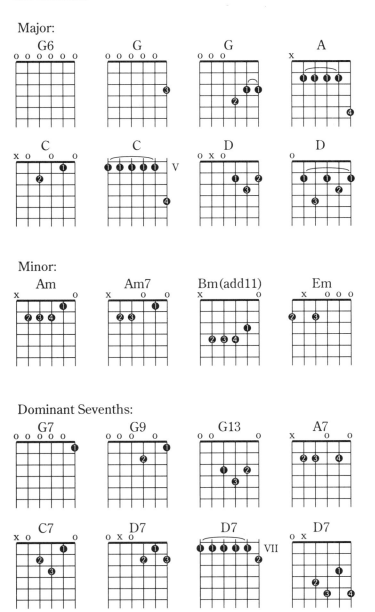

Minor:

Dominant Sevenths:

Recordings That Use G6 Tuning

As with Double Drop-D tuning, the quality of G6 recordings outweighs the quantity. Chet's version of "Yellow Bird" displays a remarkable use of an echo machine.

Chet Atkins	"Both Sides Now"
	"Yellow Bird"
	This Is Chet Atkins
	"Vincent"
	Me and My Guitar
Mark Hanson	"Devil's Dream"
	Solo Style (book/cassette)
John Renbourn	"John's Tune"
	The Hermit

Lute and Vihuela Tuning: E A D F♯ B E

Like Drop-D, this tuning alters only one string from
standard tuning. But it isn't quite as easy to use as Drop-D,
because all of the basic chord fingerings are altered.

Most classical guitarists use standard tuning when
playing the lute and vihuela repertoire of the Renaissance.
If you delve into this music, you may find that many of the
pieces are easier to play with *lute tuning*. Standard tuning
for the lute and vihuela at that time was *G C F A D G*,
which is a minor third higher than modern lute tuning for
the guitar.

There is a wide assortment of published lute music
now available in modern notation. If you haven't played
any of it, you might try to sightread a bit of it. Try playing
the pieces in both standard and lute tuning. You may
discover that some of the passages are considerably easier
to play in one tuning than the other.

Some good examples of lute music appear in Frederick
Noad's *Renaissance Guitar* (Amsco Publications). The
pieces range from easy to difficult. Noad recommends that
the player use lute tuning for a number of the more
technically challenging pieces. There is no guitar tablature
in Noad's book; only standard notation.

John Renbourn, whose playing and composing styles
incorporate many ideas of Elizabethan music, has com-
posed a number of pieces that use lute tuning. They are
available in his book *The Nine Maidens*.

To Produce Lute Tuning

You can transform standard tuning to lute tuning by
simply lowering the third string one half-step to *F♯*. When
playing standard-tuning chord fingerings, you must now
raise the third-string note one fret. For example, a first-
position E major chord now looks like a first-position A
chord (all second-fret notes) on the third, fourth, and fifth
strings.

Check your tuning by fretting the fourth string at the
fourth fret. That note should equal the open third string.
Also, the fifth-fret note on the third string now should
equal the open second string.

You might also compare the open third string with the
*F♯*s located on the first and sixth strings: The second frets
of the sixth string and the first string should each be one
octave from the open third string (sixth string: one octave
lower; first string: one octave higher).

Here's a tuning chart that points out the fretted positions used to produce lute tuning.

D Major Scale

Compare the D major scale in lute tuning with the D major scale in standard tuning. With the exception of the third string, they are identical.

D Major Scale

Common Chord Fingerings

The chord fingerings for lute tuning are similar to standard-tuning fingerings, but they require a little mental as well as physical readjustment.

For example, an E minor chord in lute tuning is fingered like an E *major* chord in standard. The first-position D minor chord is fingered like a B♭ chord in standard tuning. An E chord looks like an A-chord fingering on the third, fourth, and fifth strings. And A minor chord looks like a standard tuning D minor fingering, but here it is played on the second, third, and fourth strings.

Thus, many of the fingerings are familiar. However, you must remember which chord you want to produce.

The fingerings of some of the dominant-seventh chords are a little tricky. For the C7 chord, your little finger must reach the fourth fret instead of the third. Stretching the little finger to the fourth fret is easier if you keep your left wrist fairly low.

For the B7 chord, the little finger must reach the third string at the third fret, and the ring finger must reach the first string at the second fret. Don't worry much about these, though. You will find very few dominant-seventh chords in the lute and vihuela music of the Renaissance.

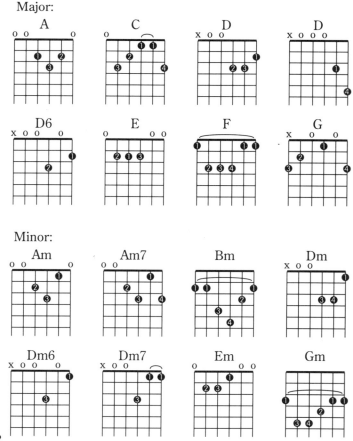

Dominant Sevenths:

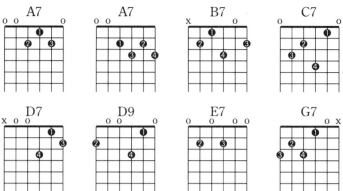

Recordings That Use Lute Tuning

Most record stores have available a good selection of lute-music performances by Julian Bream. Also, check your local music store for modern-notation anthologies.

Alonso de Mudarra	"Fantasia"
	The Renaissance Guitar (book)
John Dowland	"Fantasia"
	The Renaissance Guitar (book)
Rick Foster	"Silent Night"
	Season of Joy
John Renbourn	"Bicycle Tune"
	Nine Maidens (book)
	"Pavanna (Anna Bannana)"
	The Hermit

Additional Interesting Tunings

Of course, there are more than eight tunings that guitarists use. We have simply covered some of the more common ones up to now.

The following list offers a number of other useful alternate guitar tunings and the guitarists who use them. All tunings are listed from lowest to highest pitch. You may have to use your capo to match the pitch on some of the recordings.

Spend some time experimenting with these tunings. Begin by trying to copy the listed tunes as recorded. But take some time to find the tones of an appropriate scale and devise some chord fingerings of your own. Be creative. There are many ideas in each of these tunings.

Will Ackerman

    C G C G C E   "Townshend Shuffle"
                           It Takes a Year

    D A D F♯ A C♯   "Gazos"
                           Search for the Turtle's Navel

    E A D G C F   "Bricklayer's Beautiful Daughter"
                           Passage

    F A C C G B♭   "Childhood and Memory"
                           Childhood and Memory

    D G D F A B♭   "Processional"
                           Search for the Turtle's Navel

Keola Beamer

    C G D G B E   "Pūpū Hinuhinu"
                           Hawaiian Slack Key Guitar (book)

    D G D F♯ B D   "Kamakani 'Olu 'olu"
                           Hawaiian Slack Key Guitar (book)

    F B♭ C F A D   "Namakelua's Tune"
                           Hawaiian Slack Key Guitar (book)

Martin Carthy
    E A D E A E

David Crosby

    E B D G A D   "Guinnevere"
                           Crosby Stills and Nash
                           "Deja Vu"
                           Deja Vu
                           "Compass"
                           American Dream

    D A D D A D   "Music Is Love"
                           David Crosby

    A A D G B E   "Traction in the Rain"
                           If I Could Only Remember
                             My Name
                           "Whole Cloth"
                           Nash/Crosby

    D G D D A D   "Laughing"
                           If I Could Only Remember
                             My Name
                           "Whistling Down the Wire"
                           Whistling Down the Wire

Alex de Grassi

    D A D F♯ A C♯   "Midwestern Snow"
                           Slow Circle

    D A D E A D   "Turning"
                           Turning: Turning Back

    E C E G C D   "Window"
                           Turning: Turning Back

    E B E G A D   "Autumn Song"
                           Turning: Turning Back

Alex de Grassi (cont.)

D A D G C E♭   "Western"
                    Windham Hill Records Sampler '84

E B E G A E   "Waltz and March of the
                     Rhinoceri"
                    Turning: Turning Back

E B E G C E   "Luther's Lullaby"
                    Turning: Turning Back

Nick Drake

D G D D A D   "Road"
                    Fruit Tree

D A D G A F♯

D A D G D G

D G D G A D

John Fahey

C G C G C E   "Revolt of the Dyke Brigade"
                    Leo Kottke/Peter Lang/
                       John Fahey

C C C G C E   "Palace of King Phillip XIV of
                     Spain"
                    John Fahey, Volume 2

Peter Finger

E B E G B E   "Wishbone Ash"
                    Acoustic Rock Guitar

Michael Hedges

F A D G B E   "Lenono"
                    Breakfast in the Field

B F♯ C♯ D A D   "After the Gold Rush"
                    "Meanage a Trois"
                    Aerial Boundaries

B A D G A D   "Funky Avocado"
                    Breakfast in the Field

D A C G C E   "Layover"
                    Breakfast in the Field

D A D G C E   "Silent Anticipations"
                    Breakfast in the Field

D A D G C D   "Baby Toes"
                    Breakfast in the Field

D A E E A A   "All Along the Watchtower"
                    Watching My Life Go By

C G E G B D   "The Unexpected Visitor"
                    Breakfast in the Field

A B E F♯ A D   "Hot Type"
                    Aerial Boundaries

C G D G B C   "Rickover's Dream"
                    Aerial Boundaries

Skip James

E B E G B E   "Hard Time Killin' Floor"
                    Early Recordings, Vol. 2

Leonard Kwan

C G C G A E   "Pau Pilikia"
                    The Old Way

E A E E A E   "Ki Koalu"
                    Leonard Kwan

Joni Mitchell

C G D G B D   "Cold Steel And Fire"
                    For the Roses

John Renbourn

D A D E A D   "Pelican"
                    Black Balloon

D G D G B♭ D   "Mist-Covered Mountains of
                    Home"
                    Black Balloon

C B♭ C F B♭ F   "The Tarboulton"
                    Black Balloon

John Renbourn (cont.)

    C G C G C F   "Bourree I & II"
                        Nine Maidens (book)

Stephen Stills

    E E E E B E   "Suite Judy Blue Eyes"
                        Crosby, Stills and Nash

    E♭ E♭ E♭ E♭ B♭ E♭   "4+20"
                        Deja Vu
                        "Bluesman"
                        Manassas

Recommended Sources for Alternate Tuning Guitar Music

Recordings from many of the better-known artists included in this book (such as James Taylor; Crosby, Stills and Nash; Neil Young; or Led Zeppelin) are available from most record stores. If you haven't heard how these artists use alternate tunings, by all means buy some of their recordings and study them.

Unfortunately, a considerable amount of high-quality alternate-tunings guitar music comes from players who are not so widely known (and not as widely distributed). Sources for recordings of many of the early blues artists, as well as contemporary guitarists, are included in the following list.

I also have listed some sources of printed guitar music, including the address for back issues of the now-defunct *Frets* magazine. *Frets* published many guitar pieces from well-known and not-so-well-known fingerpickers and flatpickers. Write *"Frets* Back Issues" (see below) for a list of available issues and their contents.

Accent on Music
  Box 417
  Palo Alto, CA 94302

Acoustic Classics
  Box 1490
  Port Chester, NY 10573

Arhoolie Records
  10341 San Pablo Ave.
  El Cerrito, CA 94530

Biograph Records
  Box 109
  Canaan, NY 12029

Blind Pig Records
  Box 2344
  San Francisco, CA 94126

Edensong
  HC1, Box 101-H
  Days Creek, OR 97429

Elderly Instruments
  1100 N. Washington
  E. Lansing, MI 48901

Everett
  2020 Avenue of the Stars
  Century City, CA 90067

Flying Fish Records
  1304 W. Schubert
  Chicago, IL 60614

Folkways Records
  Distributed by Rounder

Frets Back Issues
  Box T
  Gilroy, CA 95020

Homespun Tapes
  Box 694
  Woodstock, NY 12498

Kicking Mule Records
Box 158
Alderpoint, CA 95411

Nonesuch Records
Distributed by Elektra

Origin Jazz Label
Box 85
Santa Monica, CA 90406

Private Music
220 East 23rd St.
New York NY 10010

Rounder Records
One Camp St.
Cambridge, MA 02140

Seymour Records
Box 5308
Greensboro, NC 27435

Shanachie Records
Box 810
Newton, NJ 07860

Stefan Grossman's Guitar Workshop
Box 802
Sparta, NJ 07871

Takoma Records
Distributed by Allegiance
1419 No. La Brea
Hollywood, CA 90028

Topic Records
50 Stroud Green Rd.
London, England N43EF

Tradewinds Records
Box 8294
Honolulu, HI 96815

Windham Hill Records
Box 9388
Stanford, CA 94305

Yazoo Records
Distributed by Shanachie

Tablature

There are several places on the guitar fretboard that you can play most any particular note. This flexibility provides wonderful opportunities for varying tone, but it can be a headache for sightreading standard notation. Tablature (TAB) eliminates this problem.

Tablature is a music notation system for stringed instruments that shows the performer exactly where to play each note on the fretboard. This notation is used instead of, or in addition to, standard notation, which shows the actual pitches.

If you haven't yet learned to read either system, I recommend that you first learn tablature. It's easier to learn, and it is mandatory for much alternate tuning guitar music.

The tablature system consists of six horizontal lines, each representing a guitar string. The bass string is the bottom line of the tablature staff, and the treble string is the top line.

This layout is inverted from the actual string positions on the instrument. Here, the high-pitched notes lie high on the staff and the low-pitched notes lie low on the staff. In this way tablature resembles standard notation.

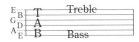

A number on a string line indicates at which fret to depress that string. The following example shows you where to pick the fifth, second, fourth, and third strings, in that order, followed by a final note that is picked on an open third string.

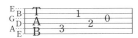

Sometimes, stems and beams underneath the staff denote the rhythm. In the example below, the rhythm is a series of eighth notes.

About the Author

Mark Hanson, formerly Associate Editor and columnist at *Frets* magazine, is a performing guitarist as well as a write and publisher. He owns and operates Accent on Music, which has published his teaching methods on the alterna ing-bass style of fingerpicking guitar. Mark also teaches guitar at his alma mater, Stanford University. Currently is working on his first solo recording, entitled *Between th Lines,* with the assistance of John Renbourn, among others.

Other Books by Mark Hanson

The Art of Contemporary Travis Picking
A comprehensive study of the patterns and variations of the modern alternating-bass fingerpicking guitar style, this book and ninety-minute audio cassette take you from the very basic patterns up through your first two solo pieces. Fourteen pieces in all.

Solo Style
A continuation of *The Art of Contemporary Travis Picking* this book and ninety-minute cassette describe the advanced picking techniques associated with some of today greatest fingerpicking professionals. There are thirteen solo instrumentals, plus "White House Blues" from John Renbourn. You'll be able to add some hot techniques and pieces to your repertoire with this package.

Recommended by Leo Kottke and John Renbourn

Available at your local music dealer or from Accent on Music.